WISDOM POWER to EXCEL in EXAM and BUSINESS

DR. MOSES AYUKETA

FOUNDING PRESIDENT OF CHRIST RESTORATION CENTER TULSA, OK, USA

MOSESENOWA@GMAIL.COM

WISDOM POWER TO EXCEL IN EXAM AND BUSINESS

ISBN: 979-8-89030-125-3 Paperback)
ISBN: 979-8-89030-126-0 (Ebook)

This book was published and printed in the United States of America by Dr. Moses Ayuketa of Christ Restoration Center, through Authorunit.

CHRIST RESTORATION CENTER

CONTACTS:

Authorunit

17130 Van Buren Blvd, Ste 238, Riverside, CA 92504

+1, 877-826-5888

www.authorunitcom

Dr. Moses Ayuketa,

1766 E. 61st Street, Tulsa, Ok 74136

+1, 9188498130

ayuketamoses@gmail.com

CONTENTS

DEDICATION

I eternally dedicate this work
to God the Father, Son, and Holy Spirit.
I also dedicate this work to those desiring to excel
in education, career, and business.

ACKNOWLEDGEMENTS

I give thanks to the Holy Spirit, my eternal, reliable, and dependable Helper. Truly no one can do this work without the help of the Holy Spirit. Also, nothing in life is ever successful without the cooperative effort of many gifted people who are willing to submit their talents, experiences, and passion for a common goal. This project is the work of many gifted people whose contributions have helped form the core of this book.

To this end, I am favored of our Lord Jesus to acknowledge the following persons: My beautiful wife Matilda, and our children Joshua and Favor for your assistance, thank you so very much, my achievements are yours;

Balbin Ekem for editing this book. May God richly reward you for your labor of love; Alice Waquoi for writing the forward of this book. May God continue to honor you.

To all my children in the Lord, I say thank you for your prayers and support, God bless you all. To all my family members, in-laws and friends, I love you, and may God bless you all.

PRAISE REPORT

ENTRANCE EXAM

In the year 1998, one of my friends and I wrote the entrance exam into ENSET - University of Douala, Cameroon. We were both successful because of the miraculous work of God. While preparing for this exam, we studied to the best of our abilities and trusted God for the rest.

In the morning of the day we were to write the main subject "Electrical Technology", which will determine the successful candidates in the Electrical Engineering department, I heard in my heart that we should restudy one of the past questions. So, I told my friend and he joined me immediately, even though time was not in our favor and we should have been concerned to hurry to class. We took time to review all questions and the answers as if we were studying it for the first time.

After the revision we hurried to the auditorium for the exam. While in the examination hall, as we flipped the question paper, it was the same past question paper we had just revised. The only thing changed was the year. We probably both scored 100% and we were successful. It was a miracle. Thank You Lord God Almighty.

BUSINESS BREAKTHROUGH

One of my sons in the faith runs a website business. For some weeks before he met me, he was having some difficulties achieving something in his business. When he met me, I knew nothing about that business but as I was praying for him, the Holy Spirit led me and I mentioned something concerning business.

According to him, after the prayer, he decided to check the transaction again. And he realized that he got a fast and easy breakthrough of what he had struggled with for several weeks to no avail. Praise God. We see that all things are always possible with God, and with anyone who can believe and obey the possibility laws that releases the corresponding Wisdom Power.

It would have been easy for him to abandon that business because of the difficulties. And if he had abandoned it, he would not have known that he could have the breakthrough. As a child of God, never abandon any idea or prayer point, until you have the practical results or hear clearly from God of what to do next.

"Wisdom Power" has been made available by the Omnipotent God, waiting for your application of the right knowledge of wisdom. The words of wisdom in this book will motivate and activate you do that stress free. So, continue to read, as you follow me in this journey, to discover the principles that will help you activate the release of Wisdom Power to Excel in all areas of life, particularly in the field of education, job and business careers.

Dr. Moses Ayuketa Enow

PRAYING FOR WISDOM

1. Pray this before and after sleep:

Holy Father fill me with the knowledge of Your will in all wisdom and spiritual understanding; that I will walk worthy of You, fully pleasing You, being fruitful in every good work and increasing in the knowledge of You. Father strengthen me with all might, according to Your glorious power, for all patience and longsuffering with joy, in the name of our Lord Jesus Christ. Thank You Father for qualifying me to be a partaker of the inheritance of the saints. (Col.1:9-12).

2. Pray this before studying a lesson:

Spirit of truth, my Teacher and Guide, teach me all I need to know as I study for the (call exam/test/interview name). Holy Spirit my Strengthener give me the strength I need to study and to get all the knowledge and understanding I need from (call subject name), in the name of our Lord Jesus the Christ. Amen!

FOREWORD

"Wisdom Power to Excel" is another example of Prophet Moses selfless and generous heart to help God's children overcome the enemies of progress; (fear, defeat and negative thinking). In this book, the prophet has provided us with scriptures, powerful prayer points and words of wisdom that if faithfully applied, will break down the barriers that stand in our way to achieving success in education, career, business, and any area of life. God said in Hosea 4:6 "My people are destroyed for lack of knowledge." This book is a must read if you desire the knowledge of wisdom to excel in any discipline or any area of life.

Many times, in my career, I have experienced the guidance and teachings of the Holy Spirit when I cried for help. I remembered in 2005, when I had just graduated from grad school, I was offered a job as a therapist at a large mental health agency in Tulsa. Apart from my grad school training, I had no prior experience in being a therapist, let alone doing the intense paperwork or navigating the humongous database. I was stressed from the pressure, taking work home and staying up late at night to get caught up on paperwork, etc.

I continued to pray and ask the Holy Spirit to help me. And one day, while driving I heard the Voice of the Holy Spirit telling me to stop in a parking lot and get out a pen and paper. I obeyed! The next thing I remembered was receiving a step by step instruction on how to do my work in an effective and efficient manner. After that encounter that day, my anxiety, fear, and stress, all went away.

I was so amazed that God even knew technology. Then Prophet Moses introduced me to the story of Daniel and his friends in Daniel 1:17. I became one of the top therapists in that agency and served there for nine years, all by the grace of God through Prophet Moses' mentorship and faithfully applying the principles he has laid out in this book. I have continued to experience so many of similar encounters with the Holy Spirit in my career and in every area of my life.

This foreword is not about me telling you my story. It is about how the biblical principles that Prophet Moses has so profoundly laid out in this book truly work and has worked for me and continue to work for me and it can do the same for you. Grab your keys to excelling in life by completely reading this book and allowing this true man of God guide your steps to excel in every area of life.

I the writer of the above foreword is, Alice Waquoi, a licensed clinical social worker. I worked as a mental health therapist for nine years in Tulsa, Oklahoma – USA. And for the past five years, I have been working with the U.S. government serving our military overseas (mainly in Asia and Europe).

Make your notes in the blank pages

INTRODUCTION

Dear reader, let me begging by encouraging us to be happy and excited for the privilege giving to us by our Maker and Owner/Lord, for His knowledge of wisdom in this book. Though everything may not look perfect according to our various expectations, bad things can still work together for our good with the help of our Maker. The Almighty in *His manifested name, Jesus Christ the Lord*, is our Maker, Owner (Lord), and Creator of the universe; He is the custodian and giver of the wisdom that brings prosperity and good success in all areas of life. With this book in your hand, you are on your way to becoming one of the wisest, excellent, and successful people in life. I congratulate you in advance.

This book, "Wisdom Power to Excel" contains; some scriptures, powerful prayer points, and words of wisdom, that if faithfully applied, will break down the barriers that stand in our way to achieving success in education, job or career, business, and any other area of life. God said in Hosea 4:6, *"My people are destroyed for lack of knowledge."* This book is a must read if you desire the knowledge of wisdom to excel in education, job or/and career, business, etc.

Wisdom Power to Excel is a book to help people be successful with excellent results in all areas of life. With this powerful tool in your hand, you will succeed in any field, no matter your age, background, past and present circumstances. I pray that God will help you to study and apply all the principles and prayers in this book.

In this book are convincing evidence and testimonies of God giving knowledge, wisdom, understanding, and excellent results, in the past, as well as today. It also contains advice on how to prepare for exams or tests, job or career and business interviews. It contains prayers for success, and also prayers against generational failure or curses and evil covenants.

God is more interested for us to have knowledge than just having certificates or titles. Therefore, start your preparations with the principles and prayers in this book, from the beginning of, the planning and completion of that; school exam or test, job or career interview, and business deal or transaction. Do not wait until few days to the starting date.

Note that: The words; "Holy Ghost, Holy Spirit, and Spirit of Truth;" all means the same person in the trinity, "God's Spirit."

This is book 1 of the series on "God's Word Practicalized"
(Dominion Formula=ASK)

CHAPTER 1

SECRET OF SUCCESS

I t is written, *"As for these four children, God gave them knowledge and skill in all learning and wisdom: and Daniel had understanding in all visions and dreams."* (Daniel 1:17).

God can give us knowledge, understanding, wisdom, with skills in all learning in the area of academic and education, job career, as He did to Daniel and his friends for their political career. He did the same to Isaac and Jacob respectively, as well as many others in the Bible, by giving them ideas that made them excel in their business career – Gen.26:11-14; 30:40-43; 31:5-13. The main secret to excel or succeed in any thing in life is, "having a good relationship with your Maker."

Our Maker knows everything, He is present everywhere, and He has unlimited power to give us whatever we need. All we need is to totally surrender and depend on Him for success in any area of life; This includes education, business, science, technology, industry, military, security, law, politics and administration, sports, music, artistic works, engineering, among others.

Then Isaac sowed in that land, and reaped in the same year a hundredfold; and the Lord = blessed him. [13] The man began to prosper, and continued prospering until he became very prosperous; [14] for he had possessions of flocks and possessions of herds and a great number of servants. So the Philistines envied him (Gen.26:12-14).

The above scripture shows that Isaac excel in farm and animal business.

"And it happened, at the time when the flocks conceived, that I lifted my eyes and saw in a dream, and behold, the rams which leaped upon the flocks were streaked, speckled, and gray-spotted. [11] Then the Angel of God spoke to me in a dream, saying, 'Jacob.' And I said, 'Here I am.' [12] And He said, 'Lift your eyes now and see, all the rams which leap on the flocks are streaked, speckled, and gray-spotted; for I have seen all that Laban is doing to you. [13] I am the God of Bethel, where you anointed the pillar and where you made a vow to Me. Now arise, get out of this land, and return to the land of your family (Gen.31:10-13).

When we read Genesis chapter 30 and 31, we see concerning Jacob, that God gave him a scientific, animal husbandry, cattle rearing business ideas, that made him excel far above Laban and many others. In this end time, God has started giving His chosen ones academic and business exploit ideas that will make them excel far above the ungodly in all national and international scenes. True Believers of

Christ (new husbandmen) will soon take over and subdue the business and political worlds among others.

It is written, *"See, I have called by name Bezalel. And I have filled him with the Spirit of God, in wisdom, in understanding, in knowledge, and in all manner of workmanship, to design artistic works and I have put wisdom in the hearts of all the gifted artisans, that they may make all that I have commanded you"* (Exodus 31:2-4,6).

The above scriptures make us to know that God gives knowledge, wisdom and understanding in all matters of life, including; political, judicial, social, medical, engineering, business, and artistic works, just to name a few. For it is written *"who has known the mind of the Lord that he may instruct Him? But we have the mind of Christ"* (1Corinthians 2:16).

True believers have a better chance to be excellent in any field of studies than unbelievers. Today, we have the New Covenant with better promises than the Old Covenant promises. Therefore, we are supposed to do better than Solomon, Daniel, Bezalel, and any Old Testament hero, because we have the mind of Christ with greater wisdom than that of Solomon.

It is written: *"The Queen of the South (Sheba) will stand up [as a witness] at the judgment against this generation, and will condemn it because she came from the ends of the earth to listen to the wisdom of Solomon; and now, something greater than Solomon's wisdom is here"* (Matt.12:42AMP paraphrased).

....

....

....

....

....

....

....

....

....

CHAPTER 2

RELIABLE TEACHER

It is written, "But the Helper, the Holy Spirit, whom the Father will send *in My name, He will teach you all things, and bring to your remembrance all things*" (John 14:26).

The only source of true wisdom and intelligence is the Almighty God. He has deposited His Spirit into all His children (true believers of Christ). Child of God, you too have been given the Spirit that will cause you to excel in any exam/test, business, career, and job, even better than Isaac, Jacob, Solomon, Bezalel, Daniel, etc. The Spirit of God is in you ready to teach you all things, if only you are willing to walk with Him as your master and final teacher, in every area of life.

The Holy Spirit is a person. Let us feel free to communicate with Him just as we do with our earthly parents. He is the only true, gentle, accurate, and reliable Helper. Pray this prayer with all your heart. In the name of our Jesus Christ; *Teach me Your way, O Lord, and lead me in a smooth path, in the name of our Lord Jesus the Christ* - (Psalm 27:11).

In time of any school test/exam, or business or job interview, the Spirit of God in you will also bring to your remembrance all things that you have studied. When you forget anything, just quietly ask Him meditatively and He will surely bring to your remembrance whatever you need.

Our Lord Jesus Christ is still saysing: *"For everyone who keeps on asking receives, and he who keeps on seeking finds, and to him who keeps on knocking, it will be opened"* (Matthew 7:8AMP).

God is always ready to give good and advantageous things to those who ask and keep on asking (asking in faith). Not just asking once or twice or thrice. Keep asking until you receive. The act of continuous asking is an act of faith.

But let him ask in faith, with no doubting, for he who doubts is like a wave of the sea driven and tossed by the wind. ⁷ For let not that man suppose that he will receive anything from the Lord; (James1:6-7).

The only question a person will ask God and not receive an answer is a selfishly motivated question. That is, asking something for a selfish gain. For it is written, *"You ask [God for something] and do not receive it, because you ask with wrong motives [out of selfishness or with an unrighteous agenda]"* (Jas.4:3AMP).

Make your notes in the blank pages

CHAPTER 3

RELIABLE GUIDE

As a child of God, whenever you are confused in any area of life particularly in time of a test/exam in school and job interview, ask the Holy Spirit to guide you. Also, if you lack business ideas and job skills, ask the Holy Spirit. And He will surely guide you into the truth of the right solution. For it is written:

"However the Spirit of truth, has come, He will guide you into all truth; for He will not speak on His own authority, but whatever He hears He will speak; and He will tell/show you things to come" (John16:13 paraphrased).

The Holy Spirit will give you understanding, and He can as well show you things to come, including the questions. That is why David said, *"I have more understanding than all my teachers, for your testimonies are my meditation"* (Psalm 119:99).

Trust in the Lord with all your heart, And lean not on your own understanding; ⁶ In all your ways acknowledge Him, And He shall direct your paths (Proverbs 3:5-6).

One of the major advantages of having the Holy Spirit in us is for Him to direct our path, so as to make right decisions, if we can acknowledge Him in all our ways. How can I acknowledge the Holy Spirit in all my ways, someone may ask? To acknowledge the Holy Spirit in all our ways is by asking Him what decision to take before making any decision, in any area of life.

If you have truly received Jesus Christ as your Savior and Lord, then you are a child of God. Therefore, always listen to your heart/spirit, because the Holy Spirit stays in your spirit. The most common channel of communication between God and His children is, "the still small voice of the Holy Spirit, as ideas in the human spirit/heart".

Talking of the "heart", I am referring to the subconscious mind. Through meditative prayers, the Holy Spirit is ready to teach us all we need to know, to guide us into all truth, and to remind us in whatever we need to be reminded of. He can also tell/show us things to come, in any area of life; just as we can see in the next chapter with the following testimonies.

Make your notes in the blank pages

CHAPTER 4

TESTIMONIES

In the previous chapter, I mentioned that God can reveal things to come. I am a living witness of this truth. There are many testimonies in my life of the work of God concerning success in school exams, as well as in job interviews. Below are a few of them.

INTERVIEW WITH OAI ELECTRONICS

In 2007, I was looking for a job in Tulsa USA as an electrical engineer. I took time and prayed about it. Few days later, I was led to Oklahoma Work Force in Tulsa. Searching in their computers, I came across a job opening with OAI Electronics Company. The job position was too low for my qualifications, but my spirit was excited about it. So, I gave them a call and went there to fill an application. I applied for that position because I was led by God to do so. I knew all things will work together for my good.

A few days later, I was called for an interview. The supervisor who came to interview me looked at my credentials and became concerned. He then asked me to hold on for him to check if there will be an opening for higher positions that would suit my credentials. He met with the manager of the Test Department who made mention of a recent opening in his department.

Instantly I was given an interview for a position in the Electronic Laboratory – Test Department. During the interview, there was a question which I could not remember the answer. As I thought on the answer, I repeated the question audibly and immediately God dropped the answer in my heart. After this question I was offered the job. Thank You Lord God Almighty.

END OF SEMESTER EXAM

In my second year at ENSET - University of Douala, Cameroon, while studying with a classmate in preparation for General Mechanics end of semester exam, on the night before the exam, I heard within me that a past exam question is going to be repeated. So, I took the past question paper and I told my friend to revise it. Simple as it sounds, he did not argue. He took time and went through the questions with their answers.

The next morning, as we went to class for the General Mechanics exam, it was the same past question paper. The lecturer just changed the year. We were both very successful, with excellent grades. My friend was very happy that God used me to be a blessing to him in that course. To God alone be the glory.

JOB BREAKTHROUGH

A lady who was jobless for a long time came to me requesting for prayers for a job. I shared with her some scriptures, particularly Isaiah 3:10 and 2Thessalonians 3:10. I told her that God has a job for her because He doesn't want us to be lazy. Then I prayed briefly with her.

A few weeks later she came back with a thanksgiving testimony of job offers from four companies. Halleluiah! Somebody who did not have a single job interview, ended up choosing from four job offers. That is the favor of God at work by faith in God's word and prayer. To God be the glory.

CHAPTER 5

POSITIVE THINKING

Let us try to always be happy and praiseful to God, not because everything is perfect as we may expect, but because with God bad things can change for our good. No matter what knocks you down in life, get up and keep going. Great blessings come as a result of great perseverance.

Your time is too valuable to waste, try to spend it well to finish your divine assignment. Do not waste your time in complains, excuses, and blame games. A person cannot fail except he/she finds what or who to blame or complain of and gives excuses for his/her failure or defeat. If you fail or you are defeated now, just say to yourself, "I did not make it this time, but I will make it next time." And with joy, prepare better for your next try.

CREATIVITY IS IN US

It is very easy to focus on the outside because that is how most people are raised in life. Our surroundings teach us to believe what we see. That is what is taught in most homes and schools.

To create, invent or renew something, one must have the ability to see what that object will look like with the eye of faith or belief before the desired outcome becomes a physical reality. Take a builder for instance, he must be able to see a building in his mind before he can design that image on paper. If God's children can see who God says they are on the inside, then it becomes much easier to become that outwardly.

We are full of the fruits of the Spirit inside of us. If we can begin accepting this truth, then we can begin manifesting it on the outside. People will always behave what they believe they are. Proverbs 23:7 says, a man will always be what he thinks of himself. If we can see what God says we are, we will eventually become what God made us to be, individually and collectively as a nation and a continent. Thank You Holy Father.

POSITIVE ADVICE

1. Talking about our problems is a waste of time. Let's talk about our successes and victories and give God our Father and Maker all the glory.

2. Good things come to those who believe, better things come to those who are patient, and the best things come to those who refuse to give up.

3. Do not pray for an easy life; pray for the strength to endure a difficult one.

4. Disappointments were not meant to destroy you but to strengthen you and help you discover better opportunities. (Meditate on 1Corinthians 10:13).

5. Sometimes good things fall apart so that better things can fall together. (Meditate on 1Thessalonians 5:18).

6. Your child will easily follow your example than your good words. Watch what you say and what you do.

7. Associate yourself with people of good quality. For it is better to be alone than to be in a bad company.

8. Don't fear change. You may lose something good, but you may also gain something better and great.

9. When you love what you have, you have everything you need.

10. The greatest act of faith some days is to simply get up and face another day.

11. Never let the things you want make you forget the things you have – Be thankful to God always.

12. Commitment means staying loyal to what you said you were going to do.

13. When you choose to forgive those who have hurt you, you neutralize the evil powers working through them against you.

14. Patience is not just waiting and doing nothing, but "constantly doing what will bring the expected results".

15. Isn't it ironic?

   - We ignore those who adore us, but adore the ones that ignore us.

   - We love those who hate us but hate the ones that love us. Let us Love all.

16. We tend to forget that joy doesn't come as a result of getting something we don't have, but by appreciating what we do have.

17. You were born to win but to become a winner, you must plan, prepare, and act to win.

18. Every story has an end, but in life every end is just a new beginning.

19.

20. Every day is a new beginning, take a deep breath and start again.

21. Know that you are loved, fearfully and wonderfully made. God brought you into this earth for His purpose, and you are an original. So, be yourself and do like Christ. Don't try to be like another man because you can never be another original or masterpiece. Be wised!

Therefore, whoever hears these sayings of Mine, and does them, I will liken him to a wise man who built his house on the rock **(Matthew 7:24).**

According to our Lord Jesus Christ, a wise person is, "whoever does His sayings. That is, practicing all that He commanded." – Matt.7:24; 28:20.

CHAPTER 6

PRINCIPLES TO EXCEL

Being defeated is often a temporary condition but giving up is what makes it permanent. Never Give Up.

OPTIMISM

NO → Shortcuts

NO → Quick fixes

NO → Blaming others

NO → I procrastinations

NO → EXCUSES!!

Being honest may not get you a lot of friends

but it will get you the RIGHT ONES. Sometimes peace is better than being right.

CONSIDER THESE IMPORTANT FACTORS

-Make sure you are saved. (Jesus is your Lord or you are child of God).

-Repent and receive forgiveness from all known sins (1John 1:9).

-Reject every spirit of fear arising from past failures. (I reject you spirit of fear! *For God has not given me the spirit of fear but the spirit of power – 2Timothy 1:7*)

-Trust God for great success and believe that you have succeeded already (*All things are possible to him/her who believes - Mark 9:23*).

-Continue to confess with the concerned scriptures, that you have succeeded.

-Do not engage in any malpractices (fraud,

bribery, corruption, etc.).

-Do not entertain any doubt and reject with sound condemnation, "all thoughts, words, dreams, and visions of failure." (Meditate on Isaiah 54:17).

-Always give thanks and praises to God for past and expected successes.

-Study hard, read your books, go through past questions, trust God and make these prayer proclamations effectively and you will surely excel.

-You can add fasting to the prayers as led by the Holy Spirit. It is very good to drink a lot of water and if possible, eat no food during the studying and writing period of any exam/test/interview. In other words, be on a daily wet fast, from the morning of the day of exam or test or interview, and break your fast after the last paper or subject of each day.

SCRIPTURAL PROCLAMATIONS

It is written: *"But there is a spirit in man, and the breath of the Almighty gives him understanding"* (Job 32:8). Therefore, there is a spirit in me, and the breath of the Almighty gives me understanding.

It is written: *"But of Him you are in Christ Jesus, who became for us wisdom from God…"* (1Corinthians 1:30). Therefore, I am in Christ Jesus who became for me wisdom from God.

It is written, *"… but we have the mind of Christ"* (1 Corinthians 2:16). Therefore, I have the mind of Christ.

It is written*: "Behold, I have done according to your words; see, I have given you a wise and understanding heart…"* (1Kings 3:12). Therefore, God has done and still doing according to my words. My Father and my God has given me a wise and understanding heart.

For by your words you will be justified, and by your words you will be condemned." (Matthew 12:37). Therefore, I can never be condemned by the words of someone else. I receive the justification for every positive word I have spoken. I cancel every negative word I have ever spoken.

CHAPTER 7

PRAYER PROCLAMATION

Start and end each prayer point with the name of our Lord Jesus Christ.

ADDRESS TO THE FATHER (LK.11:2-4)

...Most assuredly, I say to you, whatever you ask the Father in My name He will give you (John 16:23).

Thank You Lord Jesus, for giving me the privilege to ask in your name.

1. Heavenly Father, thank You for giving me the mind of Christ which cannot fail

2. I bless You Father and I acknowledge that all

wisdom and power belong to you

3. My Father my God, thank you for giving me success and victory in advance

4. I shall prevail in any exam or test by the special grace of God

5. Thank You Lord for giving me retentive memory, boldness, a sound mind and self-discipline

6. My Father fill me with the spirit of wisdom and spiritual understanding

7. My Father anoint me for success

8. Holy Father, perfect everything concerning my studies

9. My Father my God, keep me diligent in my preparations for the (exam/test)

10. Holy Father, help me to be attentive to all my lectures/lessons and exams.

11. Father I dedicate my faculties to You

12. Thank You Holy Spirit for being my Teacher, Guide and Reminder. Lord teach me all I need to know to succeed in this (exam/test/interview), guide me into all truth and remind me always of anything I forget. Thank You my Father.

SPEAK TO MOUNTAINS
(Read and meditate on Job 22:28; Matt.11:12; Mark 11:23; Luke 11:5-10; John 11:43)

"If you ask anything in My name, I will do it" (John 14:14). You can Read and meditate on Phili.2:9-11.

Start each point with, "By the authority in the name of our Lord Jesus Christ"

1. I nullify all curses of failure in my life.

2. I pull down every stronghold of failure.

3. Every pipeline/seed of failure in my life/ family be consumed by fire.

4. Every barrier and limitation to success in my life/family, break now!

5. Every inherited or self-made failure in my life, be destroyed now!

6. Every area of my life that I have lost to past failure, be restored now!

7. Spirit of failure, loose your hold on me

8. I break evil cycle of failure in my family.

9. Blood of our Lord Jesus Christ, neutralize any spell, evil word and bewitchment working against me.

10. Any strongman sitting on my success or victory be unseated now!

11. I rebuke and bind any spirit against my success and victory.

12.   I reject every satanic re-arrangement of my success and destiny.

13.   Every satanic activity in my education and career, stop now!

14.   I receive the excellent spirit of Christ.

15.   Angels of God! I charge you to minister in my favor; in all my lectures, test, exams, interviews, jobs, and businesses.

16.   I will have right answers to all questions, like Daniel.

17. I receive divine favor with all my classmates, teachers and examiners.

18.   I release myself from every spirit of confusion, forgetfulness, mistakes, and errors.

19. I receive the spirit of power and boldness, the spirit of love, sound mind and self-discipline (repeat 7x) (2Tim.1:7).

20.   I reject every spirit of fear, for my God has not given me a spirit of fear.

Thank You Father for the establishment of my decrees and the justification of my words, because of Your faithfulness to Your word (Psalms 138:2). Amen. Amen!

39

CHAPTER 8

BE SAVED

According to the New Testament, anyone who is saved is a child of God. If you are not saved, you are not a child of God and you cannot inherit the new covenant promises. If you are not saved, please make the salvation confession below, and you will be saved.

HOW TO BE SAVED

if you confess with your mouth the Lord Jesus and believe in your heart that God has raised Him from the dead, then you will be saved (Roman10:9).

When you confess with your mouth and believe in your heart that Jesus is Lord and that God raised Him from the dead, His Spirit (Holy Spirit) will start dwelling in your spirit immediately. And He will deliver you from the powers of darkness and save your life.

From that moment, you are saved, you become a child of God, as the righteousness of God in Christ Jesus. No more a sinner. You become born again and you can then see and enter the kingdom of God spiritually while you are still on earth. You will begin to have spiritual understanding of the mysteries of God's kingdom. (Meditate on Matthew 13:11; 1Corinthians 2:14).

ONLY JESUS CAN SAVE

It is written, *"for all have sinned and fall short of the glory of God"* (Romans 3:23).

It is written, *"This is* a faithful saying and worthy of all acceptance, that Christ Jesus came into the world *to save sinners, of whom I am chief"* (1Timothy 1:15).

It is written, *"And he brought them out and said, "Sirs, what must I do to be saved?"* [31] *So they said, "Believe on the Lord Jesus Christ, and you will be saved, you and your household."* (Acts 16:30-31).

SALVATION PRAYER

In accordance with Romans 10:9, I (call your name) confess that, Jesus Christ is Lord and I believe that God raised Him from the dead. Lord Jesus, come into my heart now, forgive my sins, wash me with your blood and save my soul. (eyes closed, 15seconds silence for Him to do what you asked).

Thank you, Lord, for coming into my spirit and saving my life. Now, I surrender my all to You as the Lord/Owner of my spirit, soul and body. By my faith in God's word and in Christ, I boldly confess that I am a new creature;

old things have passed away; all things have become new in my life. I am a child of God, a citizen of the Kingdom of Heaven. I am blood-washed, my sins are forgiven, and I am born again. I am now in the Kingdom of God.

I reject satan! and all his works. By God's Grace, I shall sin no more, but I shall live in righteousness forever. Thank you, Father for your love and mercy, for welcoming me back into Your Kingdom. Thank You Jesus my Savior and Lord, Healer and Physician, etc.

CONGRATULATIONS

You are hereby welcomed into the Kingdom of God. I pray the same grace that brought you into the Kingdom of Light will keep you to fulfill your destiny. I encourage you to pray and be led to a Bible-practicing church or fellowship for spiritual growth. For it is written; *not forsaking the assembling of ourselves together...* (Hebrews 10:25).

And He Himself gave some to be apostles, some prophets, some evangelists, and some pastors and teachers, for the equipping of the saints for the work of ministry, for the ***edifying of the body of Christ, till we all come to the unity of the faith and of the knowledge of the Son of God, to a perfect man, to the measure of the stature of the fullness of Christ;*** (Ephesians 4:11-13).

<u>Pray</u>: My Father, my God, my Creator and Maker, help me to discover and fulfil my purpose in this life, in the name of our Lord Jesus Christ.

CONCLUSION

Our Lord Jesus says, the Holy Spirit will guide us into all truth and he will show us things to come in future (John16:13). That means He can show questions in advanced, as we have seen in the testimonies in this book. He gives skills and business ideas. Our Lord Jesus is the same yesterday, today, and forever.

Study and pray well, and you will excel in education, job and career, business, ministry, and any other area of life. Enjoy God's grace on this journey of excellence. Try to read this book at least three times and apply all the principles and prayers. It is never too late to change for the best. Don't compare your progress with that of others, but always check with the Spirit of your Maker in you, to make sure you are doing the will of God for your life: Jesus is still saying;

"Not everyone who says to Me, 'Lord, Lord,' shall enter the kingdom of heaven, but he who does the will of My Father in heaven" (Matthew 7:21).

ABOUT THE AUTHOR

DR. MOSES AYUKETA is a multi-gifted international speaker, Electrical Engineer, Educator, and Author of many books - famous among them are "ALL Things Are Possible" and "Resurrection Power." He holds a Doctorate Degree in Biblical Wisdom from Wisdom University – Tulsa, USA, and an Honorary Doctorate Degree in Humanities from St. Thomas-a-Becket University - Canterbury, England. He holds other Diplomas and Degrees in Wisdom, Electrical Engineering Technology, and Technical Education. Dr. Moses has about seven years' experience in teaching Electrical and Electronic courses to technical education students in Cameroon. He also has some experience of working in industries, in Cameroon and the United

States.

Dr. Moses A. received a RESTORATION MANDATE with a Prophetic and Apostolic Mantle from Christ, and was ordained in the office of Apostle Prophet by the Ministerial Seminary of America. He started Gospel Ministry in 2003 in Cameroon, with a Bible Study Prayer Fellowship, followed by a radio ministry known as Mind Restoration. He is the founder of Christ Restoration Center (a ministry with a mission to spread the light), with branches in North America and Africa. He is the founder of "Africans United in Christ," and "African Future Leaders Association" (New Africa Mind Empower emancipation movement for the Restoration of African lost glory).

He organizes conferences, seminars, and crusades, particularly in United States of America and Africa. He also travels on invitations for similar assignments. He is a peace crusader and a strong donor to charity organizations, like Rainbow and Rapha

Orphanages of Cameroon. He is married to Matilda and they are blessed with three children. They are presently residing in USA, for a divine mission.

BOOKS WRITTEN BY MOSES AYUKETA

1. Practical Prophetic Prayer Praise
2. All Things Are Possible
3. Tout Est Possible
4. Destiny Programing
5. Resurrection Power
6. Possibility Power
7. Wisdom Power to Excel
8. Restoration Power
9. Unlimited Power for Success